C000175533

Paper Crusade

Michelle Penn

ARACHNE PRESS

First published in UK 2022 by Arachne Press Limited
100 Grierson Road, London, SE23 1NX
www.arachnepress.com
© Michelle Penn 2022

ISBNs
Print: 978-1-913665-67-8
eBook: 978-1-913665-68-5
The moral rights of the author have been asserted.

Thanks to Muireann Grealy for her proofreading.

Cover design: Klara Smith 2022

Printed on wood-free paper in the UK by TJ International, Padstow.

Acknowledgements

This book was inspired both by Shakespeare's play, *The Tempest*, and by *The Tempest Replica*, choreographed by Crystal Pite and performed by her company, Kidd Pivot, at Sadlers Wells, London in 2014. I was so impressed by the composition (as well the dancers' suits and masks, designed by Nancy Bryant, and the paper boats created at the beginning of the performance) that I had to create my own response — in words.

I'm grateful to Nic Stringer, Fiona Larkin, Mimi Khalvati, Kathleen M. Quinlan and Ruth O'Callaghan for their valuable feedback. My thanks also to Jill Abram.

Special thanks to Cherry Potts and Saira Aspinall at Arachne Press. It's been a pleasure working with you.

Finally, my love to Jonathan and Ralf.

Paper Crusade

On an island of perpetual sun

The Father leads a white-clad army —
banker-suits, gloves, paper masks —

in a quest
for revenge.

The Sea, offended

~ I am no mother
    bearing life ~ in my depths ~
        ~ I am black ~ opaque
          ~ keeper
            of the bones ~
            ~ bodies foundering ~
        toppled from arrogance
            burst apart like ships they sink
~ hours ~ days ~ to my deepest find ~

      ~ Humans are
          water ~ salt ~ and still they die
            drowning
        in themselves ~ sliding
     through my rawest veils
        crushed and falling
            to scrap ~ sea snow ~
until my silt ~ repose of the bones

~ I am not kind
    ~ no Mother Ocean

~ This storm I did not order
            an impertinence ~
        Screaming squalls ~ wild lightning ~ so much
            cheap noise
        A man and a boy
            flung into my reach
                torn away ~ a tease ~

~ I will watch over what I
        am owed ~ No one
            games the sea ~

Observing the storm he ordered,
The Father recalls his escape

✳

Our raft a shell   adrift
a bone flung
from crest to crest

✳

SHADES OF CONJURERS PAST:
MAKE THIS A DREAM
SEND ME EAR, AWAKE AND WARM
CRADLING THESE BOOKS, THIS CHILD

✳

(the words)
(the waves)
(the waves)

✳

My brother turned cheap thief
under loan of night
My crown   my wife in his fist
while I'm set to sea

＊

on a slap-raft, bucking, pitching
SHADES, MAKE THIS A DREAM
These frigid waves, my girl   a page
of flesh barely formed, already torn
(the words)

＊

My head rakes
the remaining oar, my cloak
a sail laden with rain
and I'm gripping my girl close
(the waves)

＊

My books skid
Find a spine, a corner, tap it twice
SHADES OF CONJURERS PAST:
TAME THESE SWELLS, BRACE US
(the waves)
Words, don't let us die

＊

The Sea listens to a tale of missing histories

~ The Daughter prods ~

> *...did you, father...? did you...? that*
> *wild sky... the sea*
> *so vehement*
> *and a ship... tell me...*

~ As always, he gazes past her
toward the horizon ~

✳

> *Calm, my girl*
> (the words)
> *The crew are safe, asleep*
> *in an intact boat*
> *never having set sail*
> *Only one has found*
> *our coast*
> *and for purpose*

✳

~ He doesn't reveal The Boy ~
　　knotted on opposite sands ~

✳

My child, it's time
you knew
Your past is a lost shore, obscured
by tongues of salt, your father
once lord over more
than rough nothings
and you a gem
formed in the pocket
of my intellect — and hers

✳

(the words)
But my books drew me deep
blinding me
to my brother lusting my place
Blood is nothing

✳

My wife, seduced, colluded
She set a storm, entranced
my troops to seek her sacrifice: us

And my magic, too fresh,
shattered

✳

A servant packed a raft
food, clothing, my books
(the waves)
By the grace
of the Shades we beached

✳

Twelve years have poured forth
I have waited, I have learned
built our Army
ordered the spirit to incite the storm
an apt escort for a thief

✳

It is our moment for justice
yours, my girl, my heir

History only bows to revenge

The Sea watches The Father at his favourite game

~ He strokes the old books
        leather fissured ~ calligraphy
               rippled ~ parchment
      crusted with salt and sand ~

            He could hurry ~ but he savours
     the wait
             opening and closing the tomes ~
                This one ~
                     sapphires spilling from pages ~
               That one ~
               emeralds ~ diamonds ~ pearls ~
                       This elixir
                       That potion

~ Book of a palace ~ Book of a wife ~
      Hair draped black
            across vellum ~ she dips ~ spins
      night silks flaring ~ arms unfolding to him alone ~

~ Then the book of The Girl
      ~ the child
     whose face he denies ~ a face
              shattered ~ in a rain
                 of glass ~

          ~ His girl ~ His heir ~ She sleeps ~

Inside a crevice of The Daughter's mind

...i am... a glorious monster...
    ...floating on the bend...
...of the waves...

      ...they guide me...   deep...
      ...to my private recess...
      ...of the sea...

...billow and curl... billow and curl...
    ...bell this suit to a dress...
        ...bulbous then slack...

...legs trail...   arms unfurl...
    hands sleeves shadows...
plunging long... fanning wide...

      ...blue-body light...   pulsing
        through... further...
          ...beyond the interfering tentacles
        of the sun...

...bulbous and billowing...
    ...i chase the capture...   the possession
        without name...
    ...gape my mouth...
      ...swish down...
        ...down...   until sound falters...

...glorious monster...

...delicate...

...dangerous...

...i am a jellyfish...

...i am the pulp of the sea...

C faces the morning's burdens

/ hunt fish spear fish chop haul stoke /
/ your f-fire f-father / / your b-breakfast /
/ i - i - i / / the h-horse / / of your best / / intentions /
/ s-saddled with your words / / you t-taught me
glass / / but I knew lightning /

/ fish spear gills bite tear scales teeth /
/ your l-lunch f-father / / your w-wine / / your
sounds / / a tied suit tight / / your ly-lying hand /
/ on mine / / fr-friend? / / no-noble workhorse? /
/ told to call / / you f-father / / but you're no /
/ f-father / / and i'm / / no s-savage / / i - i - i /

/ am the r-royalty / / of these sands / / my mother was
lightning / / i f-flared from her side / / silence our words
spacious / / wide / / her f-fire / / one jolt
scorched sand / / to clearest stone /

/ i am the b-bark / / of this place / / i am the tangled
roots / / and the t-tongue / / your sh-shades / / can they
c-catch a fish / / c-coax water from sand /
/ or the stubborn shell / / of a c-clam? /

/ chop haul stoke hunt fish spear burn /
/ your d-dinner f-father / / your s-soldier / / ready /
/ repeating your w-words / / your nothings / / if i were
lightning / / i'd burn your glass / / b-back to sand /

The Spirit laments the shapes of its debt

[twelve years
father & still i sing
a servant song]

[still i sing
a faithful song
saved from a spell-]

[bound tree & still i
sing a grateful song
a captive song   bowed]

[down by
paper wings
that never fly father]

[never bend   your
notion of what a spirit
should be?   strict folds]

[sag from this human
trap: tall   yes & muscle-
sleek but a cage]

[sexless airless
why this body?   to frame me
more in your image?]

[twelve years faithful
father & still i sing a
waiting song   you demand]

[my music
the magic
you lack   *just a few more*]

[*glorious tasks*
then i can return to sky
& so i try a wishing]

[song a wanting
song a hopeful song a
believing song]

The Boy awakens

such a hard sand
blazing white
such a brazen sun
and this sea, black shallows
sucking at my ankles
yet my leathers oddly dry
royal pearls
still hugging my neck

how far, the walls of home
courtyard servants singing?
and what of

the man, my host
and his ship?
i was his guest
goodwill child sent
the alliance now lost, splintered
with the timbers, the churn
crew clinging to currents
groping for sky
as the dome of wave
closed over, steered
each final breath

why was i spared?

what is this place, the sun
firing high, not even a shadow
to shelter beside?

The Brother, stranded

• This sea is a stranger • furious
sibling to the quiet rises of home
• waters that haven't agitated
since the night she stirred them •
My wife • His •

• This roiling sheet sought to
swallow me • suck me through its
portal • the one that dispatched
him • far • far from his impotent
throne • his chariot of the mind •

• *Read Brother Read* • *Practice*
your abstractions while I pry
apart your royal seat • *its inlay*
• *splinter of lapis* • *shard of marble*
• *a rumour* •

• *Play Brother Play* • *Exercise*
your spells while I bind you to
your chair • *Hurl you into the sea*
• *Spur the creatures to sweep you*
through waves • *long* • *deep* •

• *There Brother* • *Your chariot* •
• *There Brother* • *Your realm* •

The Father announces a grand development

✹

Army!
As your proud leader, Father
to you all
I say, Prepare!

✹

An enemy has beached
and once we revel in his defeat
my magic will be strong enough
to carry us
to my empire across the sea

✹

My people will rejoice   They are waiting
for me, for my heir, for us all
You are no longer defenders but Saviours

✳

Saviours!
A solitary page is easily torn
but fold it in half then again
Soon it's impossible to sunder
And so we are
weak each alone
but united, invincible

✳

We have been blessed!
The storm has granted two —
yes, my girl, two: the traitor
and a boy, an ally to form
We shall claim him first

✳

Come, Saviours! Our cause is just!

✳

23

The Daughter appraises what The Father landed

...this is our ally...?   this
cowering knot... shrinking scrap
...ambushed eyes jittering
to our knees... up... and...

        ...pretty
        so pretty...

a boy's jaw... barely squaring
       to a man's...
...skin unsullied... as the pearls
       embellishing his chest...
...black leathers strangely pristine...
       ...blond scruff
           glinting... a tiara
      of night... countering
father's insistent sun...

        ...this pretty thing
           could cast me...
      as woman... but...

        ...i am...
...unformed, unread...   i float
      ...at the end of my folds... pages
and corners wavering... I have been
      asleep... drugged on sun
       but I was born...

...from darkness
i long to take it... in my mouth
        once more... taste it...
...from every turn

night... the substance i seek...
        ...to flay myself
           against night...

boy... wearing your night unaware...
        wake me... envelop me...
          finish me...

The Boy encounters The Army

are further ills here to greet me?
three bodies rigid
and framed in glare, three

silent contours blazing white
box shoulders
and blade pleats
neckties and gloves immaculate
like the blankest of pages

three faces erased
by paper
facets and folds
from crown to throat

the closest, tall as a god
spreading rigid wings — wings?
yes, paper
feathers, hard-creased and sharp

beside, a twisted trunk
of a creature, waistcoat askew
one glove crisped to a claw
body a constant stutter

what is this place, land of such beings?

but — no — she
is human, human
and definitely she
trousers and jacket curving close
slender hand bucking
one hip, a girl's
defiant fidget, mask tilting curiosity

their border slides open
reveals a man
white-cloaked, face strafed
by sun
taut arrow of a beard
voice a crust enunciating my name

he knows me? but how?

no, it's not possible, that was
court lore, spells and magic
a legend implausible
yet true, solid
as the sand burning
beneath me

could i be saved?

the magician's fingers
caress a book
tap it twice

＊

SHADES OF CONJURERS PAST:
MAKE THIS BOY A SOLDIER, COMPEL HIM
TO CALL ME FATHER
FATHER OF THIS ISLAND, FATHER TO ALL

＊

and my pearls burst like seeds
my leathers unpeel
a white suit seizes me
mask folding fast
gloves impossible to pry clean

and my body pulls taut
and every protest chokes
words skid past my consent
father, i obey!

Faced with a rival, C remembers a happier past

/ so now she has / / her p-prize / / this pearly
p-prince / / so f-fine / / once i / / was that prize /
/ and g-girl / / f-father / / my finds / / their
w-words / / their words! / *repeat after me:*
seven silver swans swim silently seaward
try again: the seething sea never ceaseth

/ mornings / / on the shore / / g-girl r-rode
my back / / our defaced faces / / o-open /
/ to his sun / / her sc-scars all / / silver swans /
/ and she was / / l-laughing / / h-he was laughing /
/ g-girl and me / / two sheets / / awaiting
his crease /

/ then g-girl / / g-grew / / grown / / i o-only /
/ wanted / / it was natural /

/ chased away / / not friend / / just s-savage /

/ this f-father / / this g-girl / / and now / / this
b-boy / / g-grit lodged / / in my softest body / / i
t-torque / / my mouth / / b-bleed unseeable sap /
/ silt inside / / a hard gift /

/ this you t-taught me / / f-father /
/ defence / / against p-pain / / forms a p-pearl /

The Spirit sings to The Brother

[come stranger
come guest   lost rope from the lip
of the wreck]

[come to me
this way & here round
sands & manners]

[& behind
every tree where spells &
charms lie]

[chirp & hup
& cree & woo   spark
of mouth & aisle of light]

[this island
your luck — closer here here
stranger guest   hard —]

[played by
the fingers of the sea   erased clean
come to me   my groom]

The Brother, perturbed

• A voice • Woman's •
wavering and distant • nearing •
laughing • No • Singing •
Quick • Where is she and how
does she sound like my wife
(my precious magician come to
save me?) • But no • The voice
slides down the stifling air •
deep drone of a ship's call •
One of my crew • alive?

• No • Just the churr of a bird •
cluster of chitters and chirrups
but from where • These trees
all seem weak with heat •
stripped of leaves blank
branches singing ghosts • No •
The voice again • Human

I'm certain • and that music •
the trills and rolls of home •
Too tender for this vicious sun
And what's that there • Person?
• Angel? • No • Only glare • A
stretch of sand • Am I losing
my ground or does this island
teem with tricks?

The Father makes The Sea another enemy

✳

(the waves)
Crest, collapse, my past   *Loss*
loss, loss, she hisses   Another
slight, another slap
Crest, collapse

✳

(the waves)
(the waves)
Stay, stay, always
Spineless   Useless

✳

(the words)
I ordain eternal day
My sun wrangles the darkness
but her waters mock
deposing me   at every moment

✳

Twelve years of her farthest edge
She licked the shore
of my brother's day, he played
his prizes, imagined me
a drowned fish
(the waves)

✳

This drip of an island, I have cloistered
at its core and still I am chased
Crest   collapse
By boat or by death, the only escape

✳

(the waves)
(the waves)
(the waves)
(the waves)

✳

The Boy is ordered to rest

this flimsy pallet, my breath
a shallow sling
darkness
doesn't come
and doesn't come
sleep, my soul
trapped in white
and this crush of heat

who has stolen night?

outside, the guttering
of the man-monster
words a stutter stuck in the throat

outside, the rustle
of paper feathers
the strongman making rounds
to keep us from escaping?
or perhaps he too finds no pause

outside, the father's incantations
games of the mind
spells only a god
should throw

and the girl, sudden
somewhere
in this flagrant sun
humming
like a servant at task
her slippery lullaby
teasing palisades around me
palisades, colonnades
corridors, a chamber
my bed becomes earth, sheets
sprout new trees
leaves already claiming shade
for our bodies

The Daughter considers the status of monsters

sleep time...
>>> ...i hear him pacing... always...
>> ...scrape and lurch... hiccup of a walk...
>> ...garbled breath
>>> from behind a curtain
>>> of fronds
>>> their monster-fingers withered...

army time...
>>> ...i feel him watching... mottled body
>> twitching... cricking
>>> ...masked heat... he loiters close...
>> ...muttering *m-mine!*

he does not frighten me...
>>> ...i remember us... diving the black
>> shallows... stabbing
>>> barehanded and blind... for fish...
>> ...water fleeing the warped ridges...
>>> of his skin... my arms
>> knotted... seamed...

...i know us... hiding inside
monster hands... lobes
of leached green... then leaping...
...roaring... shocking the mice... stupefying
the insects... sending
birds scurrying to bark... horrifying
even the sands...

...why did you try to make me your island-wife...?

we live suited... masked...
as though intentions unseen...
...simply cease...

outside... he is scraping... pacing...
i hear him... always...
...monster... beyond the fingers
...of a monster...
...two monsters... playing monster... still...

The Sea takes part in a wedding of sorts

Sprinkle of sand ~ dried tendrils
    of a jellyfish ~ a curl of The Girl's
        hair pinched from between pages ~
    The Father taps
        his book ~ once ~ twice

✴

SHADES OF CONJURERS PAST:
PEEL OPEN
THIS DAUGHTER'S SLEEP
CONSIGN HER TO MY COMMAND

✴

The Girl stirs ~ rises ~ bare feet
    scuffling sands ~ Her suit slides
        into my shallows ~
            dreaming arms
        drawing close ~

    White wand
    of a girl ~ The Father's hand turns over
        and back ~ and we
        roll her ~ twirl her
        into shore and out ~ into shore and out ~

＊

SHADES!
BRING ME THE PRINCE
SOMEDAY HER HUSBAND
TONIGHT MY TRIFLE

＊

The Boy shuffles blind ~ quivering cord
  of sleep he offers
        himself ~ tie trailing ~ jacket coiling ~
        ~ He swirls beside The Girl ~ spirals
        against her ~ a masked kiss ~

    The Father's
hands clasp ~ pull apart ~ their bodies
    pleating and releasing ~
    the folds written inside them ~ across their bones ~

    ~ And I am so
        gracious ~ granting The Father this

The Boy's first day as soldier

climbing vines slide
through my gloved hands
my traps tangle
i spear no targets
cannot swim, run, drop stealthily
crawl sun-wrecked shores
or practice ambush

the girl spikes a kick, shows
a speed to beware, pointed
in her attacks
on a palm frond

the winged one
a chain of muscle, rips
dead trees from roots
battering them
against imaginary gates

— all without a wrinkle
a speck
defiling white

but the man-monster
rebels

/ i-i-i will not / / s-saviour / / for you / / f-father
of nothing / / if you're so / / m-magical / / make
a boat and / / g-go /

✳

SHADES OF CONJURERS PAST:
STILL THIS INSOLENT SAVAGE
FOR EVERY PAST SIN, MAKE HIM PAY
WITH A SLAP

✳

a flash of book
and the man-monster drops
writhing, shrieking

...father...!

...stop...!

the girl grabs the book, flings it
at his feet
sprints from the shore, jacket flapping

the father's fingers part, his eyes
fix on the wrecked one
prone and panting
still without a wrinkle
a speck defiling white

41

and i try

to run — for my life
for her
for escape
but my legs won't bend, my feet
seem one with sand, i am
trapped, rote soldier
of the book

The violence of a face

...tide pool...
...my face... straight...
one gloved finger
running the buttresses...
of my cheek... my jaw... night

of jagged rain... chaos of boots
and shouts... your arms... sweeping me
from bed... brocade abrading
my face... my last face...
...no way out but through... rain

of glass... unseated air... my flesh
laced... to hanging doors...
...the storm...

slap of oar... rain of blood
...sea trading skin for salt...
etching deep...

and now this... is your trick...
...sail us... on some paper ocean...
...to avenge...

that night... avenge
my face...

father... i am an island child...
heir to nothing... not even...
the horizon...

The Spirit faces a human temptation

[i spot him twisted &
lurching at the blistered
foot of a tree]

[rasping a broken
shell along a branch]
/ *my t-turn* / / *f-f-ather* / / *my t-turn* /

[& all at once
my hand twitches toward
the dagger fingers]

[itch for its jagged tip
& a furious funnel spins
sucks us in   together yes]

[friend   together we'll
drive our replies
into father's arrogant chest   you]

[the true royalty
our cause is just — but the spin]
goes soft   i slip back to

[wings to body not
mine   father's
faithful slave if he dies does]

[my debt die too?
will i be free or
forever marooned]

*[OH CHIRP & HUP & CREE
& WOO WOOD CURLS SCATTERED
ON THIS THIRSTING DIRT]*

*[CIRCLE & TURN
WHIP & WHIRL A DIFFERENT FUNNEL
TO DOWN*

*[THAT DAGGER COIL
THE TWISTED ONE CLOSE   OH SETTLE ON HIS
HEAD A CROWN OF SLEEP]*

C dreams of justice

/ i - i - i am not a-afraid / / not afraid / / the s-sun no
longer a t-torment / / its touch spare / / a warm hand /
/ crowning me / / i - i am a pearl / / a hard sea /
/ f-father's face a flat stone in my palm / / buckling /
/ crumbling /

/ another f-father / / words like crushed flies / / see
how they smudge / / and those books / / tear them
page page page / / feed the scraps to the sea /
/ words / / meaning l-lies / / meaning m-meanness /
/ meaning l-lies /

/ the f-fire of my mother / / lightning shocks
the sand / / blazes a d-dagger of glass / / grip it
in my fist / / pierce one more f-father / / his life
staining white / / plain blood of a plain man / / and
the g-girl / / a s-spike for her / / b-body b-bending
onto itself / / and she returns to sand / / all s-she
ever was /

/ and i - i am a tree / / s-sap spurting through my
veins / / my roots h-heave / / beneath empty huts /
/ arms unwrap to branches legs push twining trunks
and i am not a-afraid / / i am growing i am rising /
/ my leaves s-shuddering spreading / / branches and
fronds / / wind through my leaves / / the f-fire
of my mother and what is m-meant is m-meant /

46

While sleep refuses The Boy — and The Girl

sun, sun and sun
night crushed by constant day
then the searing light
dips just a trick
a footfall
her silhouette carving
white from white

boy...
        ...i guard a crevice...
        of my mind... secret
        and deep... even
my father... cannot breach it...

there... i know i'm asleep
but can change the dream... bell
        this suit... to a dress... make
myself... a jellyfish
        pulp of the sea...

                boy... you carry
        darkness... and in it...
                        ...i'm awake...

blood is nothing...

...SHADES OF CONJURERS PAST...
ACCEPT THIS STOLEN INCANTATION...
JUST FOR TONIGHT... RELEASE US
FROM ALL... OF FATHER'S FOLDS...

                              our masks slide to sand
                                   her hair tumbles
                              black cords to the waist
                    and her face — her face — silver
                                          ridges jag
                              the forehead, gouge
                                 one eye, dip flat
                                   the nose, split
                    the peninsula of her chin

see me... a monster... a ruined
*   island... go on... you will not be the first*
to deny me... his gaze...

                              no, you precious thing
                                    so ravaged, so
                    ravishing i hold no questions
                              closer, only closer

his mouth... twinning...
    twining... bulbous
        and billowing...

                — and she's stinging
              engulfing lips, cheeks
                pillaging creature
                     her skin
          long sugar to the tongue

my love... my prey...
i am ...translucent...
        ...truculent
            darken me...

While sleep refuses The Father

✳

Safe, barricaded inside sun, I should be
but my enemies stir my soldiers
our girl
Oh, my lost wife
Even my own light turns cruel

✳

Once — our corners and pages
You, murmuring your latest find
You, your intellect
pressing into me, night silk casting winding turning—
My grateful incantations
dipping you down, your hair draping black
Every spell   You, my true study

✳

(the words)
The fine eddies of your words
You, the greatest illusionist
the most perfect thief
and I, so naïve   I reeled

＊

into your darkness
turning, turning
while you cast beyond my shoulder

＊

Our child, I have stifled her — Well, I have tried I
cannot topple a second time, to a second
woman   Her body turns, searches   I sense it
Her skin is restless

＊

C wakes and overhears the lovers

/ m-m-mine! / / she is a sweet sweet root / / i - i
t-taste her / / on the dust / / m-mallow melting /
/ my tongue / / her spine / / a s-soft switch bending /
/ yielding / / but she feeds her / / self to that / / int-
interloper / / his perfect measures / / while i am /
/ too many / / crooked lines /

/ to d-drag her / / between my teeth / / s-suck that
marrow / / crush that root / / g-girl i will
consume you / / pound that marrow through / / leave
myself behind / / m-me and all my crooked lines /

/ oh you'll resist / / true s-soldier / / spinning kicks
landing fists i know / / but n-no / / she succumbs slips to
mercy /

/ c-claw away the mask / / g-grasp the scarred child /
/ her face / / silver lines glinting / / split her s-suit /
/ the firm rise / / of knitted s-skin / / glinting
like fins / / pale / / undefiled / / a f-fish never before /
/ hooked /

/ she s-surges / / stranded hands / / r-reining my
hair / / legs clamping my back /

/ to s-suck her down / / make that b-body ripple /
/ a fish fighting the sky /

The Spirit lures The Brother to The Father's shore

[chirp & hup
& cree & woo   come   stumble
through this scrub   this sun   come to me]

[i am your music
the trills & beats you miss
power symmetry & pulse   i am]

[your magician   the one
you thought forever lost
i am your throne & your]

[realm   waiting
come in hope   in weakness   in desire
in wanting   come]

[in ambition
& manoeuvre   in anger
& treachery   come in lover & in king]

[the shore your altar
& your port   once again be the groom
of your own sun]

The Brother: An inconceivable reunion

• Mirage • He is a mirage •
and still a shiver grips me •

My servants lied • I should have
demanded his head • And
the girl's •

• This island has not been kind
the beard trailed white • the eyes
tarnished • but a voice of air •
as though he has greeted me daily
• *Brother, what news of my*
realm? My wife? Twelve years
carried — is all well?

• Yet he calls for no answer •
White sweep of cloak • Black glass
of a stare • He strokes a tome •

• The sea showed a grudging
mercy • Will it spare me twice?
A risk • a rush toward shore • my
luck • maybe •

✳

SHADES!
TRAP HIM, SHACKLE HIM TO SAND
STEAL HIS SCHEMING TONGUE
SEAT HIM ON HIS FINAL THRONE

✳

• I am snared muted • enraged •
• At the command of a mirage •

The Army and The Brother face off

~ Flat sand his beggar's bench
        The Brother gapes
                at a wall of white
        masked phantoms
                        stepping close ~

The Daughter:
...he knows me...
        quick tip of the head... ticking me
off his list... blood
        that sought my blood...
        ...thief... wearing my father's face...

                ...this is meant to be... my moment... ours...
                but who here... is the greatest monster?

C:
/ s-same hands / / s-same beard / / same disdain c-carving /
/ the planes of his f-face / / who can tell f-foe / / from f-foe? /
/ might as well / / s-separate waves / / from the s-sea /

The Spirit:

[even an enemy, even
a magician is merely a turn
of tendon around bone, a spurt]

[of blood, a few lists
of skin holding   a short
crack of power]

The Boy:

the man from the ship
once my host
i have nothing to avenge
no war with him
i am dead, drowned
only hers

~ Flat sand his beggar's bench
The Brother sits high
defies the wall of white ~

~ The Father hears
~ *Loss loss   Cowardice*
He raises a book ~
a hand ~

The Father confronts his mirror

＊

His face my face, his eyes
mine, his fists

Face, eyes, fists— a defiant horde   After
all his crimes, he is not sorry
(the words)
No words pass, not one

＊

Spells surge, tempests
and temptations
Sun, scathe his eyes, slash
him to paper lace —
Waves, marry him, make him
your shuddering fish, I dare you —
Blood is nothing

＊

His face
my face, his blood
mirrors back
words and waves
(the waves)

＊

Revenge a shell of dust
burnt by
empty sun, my

＊

hand grips his   He smiles
smiles, he knows

＊

A single pulse, my hand to his
(the words)
(the words)
Mercy does not   confer forgiveness
yet I   surrender him
with a single breath

＊

watch him rise
conjure a cloud to catch him
— now a worm, now a serpent, now a dog —
demon fit for his kind —
Your waves, Brother
Your chariot

＊

The Father's reckoning

*

Paper raft, paper wreck
By boat or by death

*

My island
I, Father of so little, a clutch of
soldiers under duress
and their conspiracies
Everything turns, everyone

*

The sea batters the sand
She offers   no gruff embrace
Her waters fall away
repulsed

I am neither loved nor feared, so what remains?
Justice!
But whose?
Whose?

✳

The black sea swells
one taunt, another, always another
Another slight, another   slap
                    She has not forgotten
          the boy and my brother
two storm-bodies   I withheld
                    and she's hissing, *Innocence*

✳

          She's hissing
     Sacrifice   By boat
               and by death

✳

His enemy spared, The Father addresses The Army

✱

Once, I folded
a paper boat   and it looked like
a crown, my   crown

Any page can be bent
every word and image
playing slave to ambition, pride
(the words)

Spirit! Workhorse!
Come close, closer!

✱

Spirit
(the waves)
For every weight you bear
I could order a storm
soak you free like so much   paper

But an arid spell
is best
for this thirsting island

✺

SHADES, RELEASE THE BURDEN
OF THIS BODY, THESE WINGS
RETURN THIS PAGE OF STARS
TO ITSELF!

✺

And you, Noble Workhorse
I embrace you   as brother
if not by blood then by words
(the words)

SHADES, RESCIND THIS SUIT!

Look, your ruttled skin

SHADES, RETRACT THIS MASK!

I forgot — your eyes   are blue and
your hair, how it unwinds to your knees

✻

Noble Brother, we are leaving you
All of us
It is time
When darkness   strikes your eye
we'll be far
but for now

✻

take my hand   just once
embrace me
Forgiveness is dry

✻

C offers no reprieve

~ He levels a stare ~ lurches away
        from The Father ~
                The Boy ~ and The Girl ~

                                    ~ The Girl ~

                hobbles far
                        to the island's quietest reach ~

        where he bathes ~

The Spirit sings its own song

          blare of light my sky
surges open sweeps
me up & in breathier airier

          i stretch
every star of my stars   spread
& mesh with all spirits

          in song no mortal ear
can trace   absorbed once more
inside the flesh of the sky

          yet a single glance
at the island
his delirious sun

          & i fear
the marked moments
to come

The folding

✳

Once, I folded
a paper boat   and it looked like
a crown

✳

Now, this page
plucked   from a book

Fold it in half
and again

✳

Tug corners to
a triangle

Raise
a mast of paper
and hold it high

✳

Is the sea laughing
or is it my sun?

✳

The ceremony

✳

Come, children, to shore
Yes   together
Trade suit and mask
for robes: leather, pearls
lace and gems

Accept
this gift
this paper boat

✳

SHADES!
I CAST MY GREATEST SPELL
CHANGE THIS FOLDED PAGE
TO A TRUE VESSEL

✳

My girl, my boy
I will not sail at your sides
but we
will meet again

✹

Let me help you both aboard
Here, water, food   Here, silks
to shield you from sun

and here, my
most precious volumes

They know
where to go

✹

The Sea joins the voyage

~ The lovers begin to dream ~
        The Boy's land ~ or perhaps
           The Girl's
      to avenge her place ~
              Possibilities
so lush ~ so bright ~ they practically blind

  ~ But the books
      dip the boat down ~ ride it
          heavily in my tides ~ The Girl's eyes
      horrify ~ The Boy cries out ~ They seize
        the oars ~ fight to leap free ~ but
        rope binds wrists ~ ankles ~
          betrothing them to wood

~ The Girl's robes bloat
    The Boy's pearls eddy down ~
      The Father turns away

    while the books spring wide
           ~ and I
              reach up to read

How a book dies

＊

Atop the waves it drifts
Days and days
the leather bends
the pages hang   willowing
in the currents

＊

The sea turns the tome in her fingers
flicking a corner, wavering
a page   Small fish ride the lines
nibble, nudge the spine
softer along

＊

Black waters press close
The binding gives
stitches fall stray, scraps
of white tumble   blind
snow of spells, pulp of the sea

*

Two were plucked from your arms, two
returned: parity   Yet I offer extra penance
fold myself from this shore
My body for a book, my blood
for salt

SHADES OF CONJURERS PAST:
I SNUFF OUT THIS SUN, CALL
TO THE DARK
CAST MYSELF UPON THIS SLEEP

*

(the words)
(the waves)
(the waves)

*

The Sea, fatigued

~ Day upon day I paint you ~ your portraits
    across these rocks ~ your
        lofty faces ~ so singular ~ so deserving
    ~ I paint you in froth
        watch you dry ~ evaporate
                to salt ~

~ Year upon year I wrap my water
    around my water
        unsilt the bones ~ stripped innocent ~ white ~
        ~ every ship down ~ the faces ~ the
            flailing inside
        my glassiest licks

~ Sometimes I imagine I am The Girl
    whisper ~ *I am unfinished* ~
        darken me ~ I dream
    of plunging deep
        inside myself ~ dissolving ~

I am no mother ~
I am continuous ~

~ I paint ~ I watch ~ I embrace the souls ~ waiting
        for sea snow
                and the settling of bones

        ~ But I'd rather consign them to the sands
My body longs
        for greater sport ~

C celebrates his losses

/ hut leaf roof floor wall branch twig / / i spit father / / i laugh / / hunt fish spear fish chop haul stoke / i hunt you now / burn you books books words spells tricks lies lies / they are gone go ____ / back to your lands of glass / i am not afraid

girl i forget your face your form / father your
spells / and what was that name / you gave me? / sav____
/ sav____? i forg____ ha! father fading / his books those
sounds fath far fa____

now nothing pushes out a name / every spot of sand mine mine! i am not afraid / / words? slivered swinging skyward something? s____? ha! i forget!

swans slicing sun to cloud soft rain / parched vines drink high the sky stretches to itself again fades frees to black / sweet dirt slow moon and stars
and stars st____ and i am not af____

//

/

About the Author

Michelle Penn is a dual UK/US national. She lived in Paris for many years before moving to London in 2005. Michelle plans innovative poetry/art/music events in London as part of Corrupted Poetry. She's also a member of Malika's Poetry Kitchen.

Michelle's debut pamphlet, *Self-portrait as a diviner, failing,* won the 2018 Paper Swans Prize. Her poetry has appeared in numerous publications, including Popshot, The Fenland Reed, Shearsman, Magma, Under the Radar and Butcher's Dog.

Several of Michelle's poems have been performed as part of Arachne's Solstice Shorts Festivals, and published in their respective anthologies, including *The End of Ramadan,* performed at Ellon, at Dusk on the 21st December 2017 and published in the anthology *Dusk*; *Precarious,* performed at Edinburgh and London, at noon on the 21st December 2018 and published in the *Noon* anthology; *The Sinking of Mrs Margaret Brown,* performed at Greenwich and Maryport, and published in the *Time and Tide* anthology; and *Retablo For the Deep Ocean,* performed online and published in our 2021 Solstice Shorts anthology, *Words From the Brink.*

More Poetry from Arachne Press

A Pocketful of Chalk Claire Booker
ISBN 978-1-913665-69-2 £9.99 (July 2022)
The South Downs lie at the heart of this collection – the sunsets and huge skies, cliffs and fossils, fishing vessels and windmills, people and sheep. Past, present and future collide within geological and emotional landscapes. Claire Booker offers moving and memorable poetry from an iconic corner of England.

A Voice Coming From Then Jeremy Dixon
ISBN: 978-1-913665-40-1 £9.99
[CONTENT WARNING]
Starts from Jeremy's teenage suicide attempt and expands to encompass themes of bullying, queerphobia, acceptance and support. Includes unexpected typography, collage, humour, magic, discotheques and frequent appearances from the Victorian demon, Spring-heeled Jack.

This Poem Here Rob Walton
ISBN: 978-1-913665-30-2 £8.99
When Rob Walton went into lockdown, he didn't know that he would also go into mourning. Here he writes about the life and death of his dad, and how sadness seeped into various aspects of his life.
He also manages to find cheap laughs, digs at the government, celebrations of the young and old, unashamed sentimentality and suddenly disarming moments of tenderness.